WELCOME TO TRANQUILITY

ONE FOOT IN THE GRAVE

MAY   2012

WELCOME TO TRANQUILITY

ONE FOOT IN THE GRAVE

GAIL SIMONE
Writer

HORACIO DOMINGUES
Artist

JONNY RENCH
CARRIE STRACHAN
Colorists

TRAVIS LANHAM
Letterer

NEIL GOOGE
JOHNNY RENCH
Cover Artists

ETHAN VAN SCIVER
MOOSE BAUMANN
Variant Cover Artists

Ben Abernathy
Editor – Original Series

Kristy Quinn
Assistant Editor – Original Series

Ian Sattler
Director Editorial, Special Projects and
Archival Editions

Robbin Brosterman
Design Director – Books

Eddie Berganza
Executive Editor

Bob Harras
VP – Editor in Chief

Diane Nelson
President

Dan DiDio and Jim Lee
Co-Publishers

Geoff Johns
Chief Creative Officer

John Rood
Executive VP – Sales, Marketing and
Business Development

Amy Genkins
Senior VP – Business and Legal Affairs

Nairi Gardiner
Senior VP – Finance

Jeff Boison
VP – Publishing Operations

Mark Chiarello
VP – Art Direction and Design

John Cunningham
VP – Marketing

Terri Cunningham
VP – Talent Relations and Services

Alison Gill
Senior VP – Manufacturing and Operations

David Hyde
VP – Publicity

Hank Kanalz
Senior VP – Digital

Jay Kogan
VP – Business and Legal Affairs, Publishing

Jack Mahan
VP – Business Affairs, Talent

Nick Napolitano
VP – Manufacturing Administration

Ron Perazza
VP – Online

Sue Pohja
VP – Book Sales

Courtney Simmons
Senior VP – Publicity

Bob Wayne
Senior VP – Sales

SALEM STATE
MAXIMUM SECURITY
PENITENTIARY

AND COVER THY NAKEDNESS.

IT'S TIME,
MAYOR.

DIDN'T THINK IT'D BE SO SOON.

SYSTEM'S LIKE THAT, SOMETIMES.

YOU KNOW, I'M REAL REAL SORRY ABOUT ALL THIS.

I MEAN, IT'S A STAIN ON YOUR GOOD NAME, MAYOR.

GOTTA CUFF YA. REGS.

YOU'VE BEEN GOOD TO ME, SGT. LOPEZ. I APPRECIATE IT.

BUT IT'S NO MORE THAN I DESERVE.

ONE MAN'S WALLET, 47 DOLLARS IN BILLS, ONE BLACK SHIRT, ONE WHITE SUIT, ONE "MASK..."

EXCUSE ME. MAY I...

MAY I WEAR THE MASK?

DON'T LET US LEARN YOUR NAMES

TODAY? YOU DO WHAT YOU WANT, MAN.

THAT'S HOW IT GOES.

AH. I'M READY.

WELL, THAT'S NICE, GETTIN' A HERO'S WELCOME. WHAT WAS THAT HEROIC THING HE DONE AGAIN?

OH, YEAH, ATTEMPTED MURDER.

THE LITTLE DICKENS.

I SAW COLLETTE IN THE CROWD.

YEAH?

"WELL, THEN MAYBE THIS *WEREN'T* A WASTED TRIP, AFTER ALL, SHERIFF."

...HOW WAS THE *CHOW*, MAYOR?

ANXIOUS TO GET BACK TO YOUR WIFE'S CHICKEN AND DUMPLINS, I IMAGINE!

...MEAT LOAF. IT'S HER MEAT LOAF I MISS.

AN' MISTER, YOU HAVE NO IDEA.

COLLETTE?

MAYOR?

HERE COMES *SOMETHIN'*, I BET YA A BISCUIT.

...

NO BET. BE PREPARED, CASE SHE'S GOT A *GUN*.

WE SHOULD BE SO LUCKY.

...CAN SEE, BEHIND ME IS A SCENARIO NONE COULD HAVE IMAGINED SCANT WEEKS AGO, AS THE VERY JOURNALIST WHO ACCUSED ALEX FURY, AKA MAYOR FURY, OF ATTEMPTING TO *KILL* HER IS NOW EMBRACING HIM AS ONE WOULD A LONG-LOST *FATHER.*

"THIS IS ONLY THE *LATEST* IN A SERIES OF SHOCKING TURNS IN THIS CASE, THAT HAS CALLED INTO QUESTION THE COMPETENCE OF THE TRANQUILITY SHERIFF'S DEPARTMENT. *DID* THE LOCAL POLICE RUSH TO JUDGMENT AND JAIL A MAN UNFAIRLY?"

I'M SORRY. I'M SO SO SORRY. IT'S ALL MY FAULT.

MISS PEARSON... I...I...

I HAVE TO GO.

"AND WHAT *OF* THE FORMERLY RESPECTED MS. PEARSON? WHAT WOULD DRIVE HER TO MAKE SUCH A CHARGE AGAINST ONE OF AMERICA'S MOST BELOVED WAR HEROES? AND WHY WOULD SHE *RETRACT* THAT STATEMENT SHORTLY AFTER THE TRIAL BEGAN?"

"THE PROFESSIONAL CAREER OF MS. COLLETTE PEARSON IS *OVER.*"

SMILE FOR THE CAMERA!

JUST ONE MORE PHOTO...

CAN YOU MAYBE *KISS* MS. PEARSON, SHOW THERE'S NO HARD...

JUST ONE MORE

JUST ONE

JUST ONE MORE QUESTION

GUYS, PLEASE. STOP.

FORGIVE ME.

"SOME HAVE MADE ALLEGATIONS OF A SORT OF *FATAL ATTRACTION* SCENARIO. OTHERS SAY THE MAYOR MADE A BRIBE FROM HIS CONSIDERABLE FORTUNE. BUT MOST IN THE INDUSTRY AGREE..."

MY. WHAT A *LIST* OF CHARGES AGAINST MY CLIENT.

SHERIFF, I WONDER...

DID YOU ACTUALLY *SEE* THE DEFENDANT TRY TO INJURE MS. PEARSON?

WELL, NO. I MEAN, I WASN'T THERE AT THAT *MOMENT.*

DID YOU HEAR HIM *THREATEN* HER IN ANY WAY?

THE SUSPECT'S *BODY* LANGUAGE INDICATED...

SHERIFF LINDO. DID YOU *HEAR* A *THREAT.* ANY THREAT AT ALL?

... NO.

NOT *EXACTLY.*

WE ARRIVED JUST *AFTER,* I GUESS.

NO. NO.

WELL, NO. NOT IN SO MANY...

LISTEN. SHE WAS *SCARED.*

DID YOU SEE HIM *HIT* HER, MISS...ER... "MANGACIDE?"

...NO.

NO. HE NEVER THREATENED ME.

BUT MISS *PEARSON.* YOUR PREVIOUS *TESTIMONY*--

--WAS A LIE, COUNSELOR.

I'M TELLIN' YA 'CAUSE I KNOW YOUR MAMA WON'T, LEONA. SEX ALONE? IT'S NOT ENOUGH.

ONE AND A HALF POUNDS GROUND BEEF, HALF A POUND GROUND PORK.

SPLASH OF WORCESTERSHIRE, HALF TEASPOON OF SALT.

HALF TEASPOON OF PEPPER.

UM. WHAT DO YOU MEAN, NOT ENOUGH?

LOTTA WOMEN CAN MAKE WHOOPIE.

NOT ALL OF 'EM CAN COOK. 8 OUNCES TOMATO SAUCE.

YOU MEAN, THIS MEAT LOAF RIGHT HERE WILL KEEP A GUY FROM...

HONEY, HE GETS THIS TWICE A MONTH, HE WON'T BE TRYING ANYONE ELSE'S RECIPES, UNDERSTAND? TWO RAW EGGS.

HERE'S THE SPECIAL PART...TWO HANDFULS OF OLD-FASHIONED OATMEAL, UNCOOKED.

UNCOOKED OATMEAL, GOT IT.

ONE MEDIUM YELLOW ONION, DICED. THEN THE FUN PART.

YOU DON'T USE A SPAT FOR THAT? OR A MIXER?

GIRL, THIS AIN'T ABOUT COOKING. THIS IS ABOUT MAKING LOVE.

THEN YOU SHAPE IT. YOU SEE WHAT I'M GETTING AT HERE?

I...I THINK SO.

IT'S...IT'S KINDA INTIMATE, ISN'T IT?

IT IS. COOKING FOR CUSTOMERS, THAT'S ONE THING.

COOKING FOR YOUR MAN...

WELL, YOU SAVE YOUR SPECIAL FLAVORS FOR HIM, RIGHT?

THE GLAZE IS JUST AS EASY. FOLLOW ME ON THIS...

OKAY, THE MEAT LOAF GOES IN THE OVEN AT 350 DEGREES FOR ONE HOUR.

350 FOR AN HOUR, GOT IT.

DON'T YOU LET IT COOK NO MORE'N THAT, LEONA. OR EVERYTHING I SAID GOES WRONG *DOUBLE*.

UM. YOU KNOW...

...I MIGHT LIKE TO KEEP A GUY MYSELF SOMEDAY, YOU KNOW, MAYBE A LITTLE.

SOMEDAY?

MANGACIDE, DEAR, YOU AREN'T QUITE *READY* FOR *THIS* RECIPE.

COME BACK WHEN YOU HAVE A BABY IN THE OVEN, HONEY.

SPEAKIN' OF HONEY, JUST A SQUIRT'LL DO. JUST LIKE A MAN!

MISSUS *SUZY FURY!* HOW ABOUT A LITTLE *DECORUM* OR SOMETHING?

THAT WAS NEVER MY STRONG POINT, LEONA. 1/8 TEASPOON SALT, A TABLESPOON OF BROWN SUGAR, HALF CUP TOMATO SAUCE...

MS. F... I MEAN, SINCE YOU BROUGHT IT UP, AND ALL.

SUZY. HOW COME...

HOW COME YOU AND THE MAYOR NEVER HAD ANY KIDS?

OW! WHAT WAS *THAT* FOR?

NOSEY PARKER!

THAT'S NOT OUR BUSINESS.

IT'S ALL RIGHT, LEONA. SHE DIDN'T MEAN ANY HARM.

WE HAD A CHILD, GIRLS.

WE LOST HIM.

SUZY...!

OH. OH, NO. I...

I'M SUCH AN *IDIOT.*

STUPID ROCKET LAMEBRAIN GEAR FLUFFHEAD!

NO, NO, HONEY. YOU COULDN'T KNOW.

IT'S NOT RIGHT TO... I MEAN, I HAVE NO RIGHT TO LIVE IN THE PAST LIKE THAT.

LISTEN. WITH THE TWO OF YOU AND YOUR BAND GOING ON THIS BIG TOUR TO JAPAN, I'M LOSING *BOTH* MY BEST WAITRESSES. SO LET'S SAVE THE TEARS FOR GOODBYE, HUH?

SUZY, I WOULD *NEVER* MEAN TO...

HUSH. I KNOW, PUNKIN.

CAN'T FACE MY HUSBAND'S COMIN' HOME PARTY WITH A FACE LIKE *THAT*.

ANYTHING I CAN SAY TO SEE THAT SMILE COME BACK, SUNSHINE?

UM...

TEACH ME TO BAKE PIES? THAT LEMON CHIFFON ONE?

NOW *THAT* IS SEXY COOKIN' *ADVANCED*.

AND YOU AIN'T *NEAR* READY.

MIX THE GLAZE WELL, PUT IT ON THE COOKED LOAF (BUT LEAVE A LI'L EXTRA FOR DIPPIN'), THEN STICK THE WHOLE CABOODLE BACK IN THE OVEN FOR ANOTHER FIFTEEN AT THE *MOST*.

YOU GOING TO THE MAYOR'S... TO *ALEX'S* COMIN' HOME PARTY, HENRY?

WELL, HIS PARTNER KILLED SEVERAL PEOPLE, INCLUDING MR. ARTICULATE, THE ONLY MAN IN TOWN BESIDES MYSELF WHO KNEW HOW TO PLAY *CHESS* PROPERLY...

AND HIS GOOD FRIEND *TRIED* TO KILL *ME*. MY TESTICLES *STILL* HAVE PLIERS MARKS ON THEM!

OF *COURSE* I'M NOT GOING.

HMM. YES, YES, THAT'S THE *PRINCIPLED* THING.

SUZY'S CATERING THE WHOLE THING HERSELF, I HEAR.

GOT A CAKE GOING THE SIZE OF *MONTANA*.

A CAKE, YOU SAY?

MMM. FIZZY CHOCOLATE CHERRY, IF THE SCUTTLEBUTT IS TO BE BELIEVED.

HM. WELL. GOOD FOR HER, THEN. I HOPE YOU *CHOKE* ON IT, MR. BIG TIME SUPERHERO CLOD!

DIRTY 'TATERS AND BROWN BEEF GRAVY, TOO, I HEARD A RUMOR.

CURSE YOU, MAXI MAN!

I'LL GO.

I WOULDN'T. AIN'T NO CAKE *TASTY* ENOUGH TO FACE THE BIT OF HELL THAT MAN GOT COMIN'.

WHAT THE HELL?

COME WITH ME. THERE'S NO TIME.

YEAH, THAT'D BE GREAT!

OH, AND A RAT FOR MY SNAKE!

RIGHT AWAY, MISTER ZEKE!

EVERYBODY, HUSH FOR A MINUTE. *SHHH!*

LISTEN.

YOU ALL KNOW MY HUSBAND. AND I AIN'T GONNA LIE TO YOU.

YOU ALL KNOW HE *DID* WHAT THEY SAY.

I'M NOT ASKING YOU TO FORGET.

BUT YOU ALL KNOW HIM. YOU KNOW THE GOOD HE'S DONE.

I'M JUST ASKING THAT WHEN HE WALKS THROUGH THAT DOOR...

CLOSED FOR A SPECIAL COMING HOME PARTY

BY INVITATION ONLY

WE'D LOVE TO SEE Y'ALL COME BACK THOUGH!

...THAT YOU ALL REMEMBER A LITTLE BIT OF KINDNESS.

FOR ME, IF NOT FOR HIM. ALL RIGHT?

EVERYONE CLEAR ON THE PLAN, THEN?

UM. SUZY.

SUZY!

WHAT, MANGACIDE? WHAT *IS* IT?

THE *TRUCK!* WE HAVE TO GO *BACK.*

HUH. "STRONGEST MAN ON EARTH."

HUH? WAIT.

LISTEN, WHO *ARE* YOU? I'VE HAD JUST ABOUT ENOUGH OF THIS, YOUNG MAN. THOSE PEOPLE COULD BE *HURT,* AND WE'RE JUST...

"STRONGEST MAN ON EARTH," RIGHT?

LOOKA THAT MOON, WOULD YA?

I'M AFRAID I DON'T QUITE...

THAT'S WHAT THEY *CALL* YOU, YEAH? THE PRESS AND LIKE THAT. THE "FANS."

YEAH. THAT'S WHAT THEY CALL ME.

YOU DON'T WANT TO TANGLE WITH ME, BOY. THAT'S A NATURAL BORN *GUARANTEE.*

OKAY, NO MORE ZOMBIE TESTS, GUYS, OKAY?

LET'S LET THE MEDICAL EXAMINER GIVE HIM A ONCE-OVER.

YOU MIND, DR. STEEL?

NO, TROY, BUT I HAVE TO SAY...

...I ONLY GIVE *MOST* PEOPLE *ONE* AUTOPSY.

THIS'LL BE *THIS* BIRD'S *THIRD.*

THIS WON'T HURT, MR. A.

I COULDN'T REFUSE YOU IF IT DID, DEAR LADY.

HUH.

THIS IS WEIRD.

WHAT'S WEIRD, RACHEL?

WHEN HE WAS KILLED THE *FIRST* TIME, HE WAS RIDDLED THROUGH WITH CANCER, DEPUTY VERRILL.

METASTATIC CANCER LEAVES LESIONS ON THE BONES. LIKE SWISS CHEESE.

HIS BONES ARE STRONG AND SOLID, NOT MOTH-EATEN AT ALL.

BONES, LIVER, LUNGS... NO LESIONS.

THE LUNGS SHOW NORMAL INSPIRATION AND EXHALATION AND HIS HEART IS BEATING STRONGLY, THOUGH IT STILL SHOWS THAT SLIGHT SINUS ARRHYTHMIA HE'S ALWAYS HAD.

CAN'T IMAGINE AN IMPOSTOR GOING TO THE TROUBLE OF FAKING THAT LAST BIT.

THERE ARE PERISTALTIC WAVES IN THE INTESTINES, DENOTING A FUNCTIONING GASTROINTESTINAL TRACT. I CAN SEE THE FORMATION OF RED CORPUSCLES IN THE BONE MARROW.

THAT'S THE CAPPER, TROY. THIS MAN IS A GOING CONCERN, IF YOU GET MY DRIFT.

HE'S ALIVE, AND HE'S THE REAL *THING*.

WELL, IT'S ALWAYS NICE TO HAVE ONE'S AFFAIRS IN ORDER IN MATTERS OF LIFE AND DEATH, I FIND.

YOU AIN'T OUT OF THE CLOUDS YET, MR. A.

I SAW YOUR CORPSE. GONNA TAKE A LOT OF CONVINCING FOR ME TO START INVITING YOU TO PARTIES AGAIN.

HENRY? YOU LOOK LIKE YOU HAVE SOMETHING TO *SAY*.

HMMM?

OH. NO. NOTHING SET IN STEEL, MAXI-MAN.

BUT IT'S NOT AS IF SUPPOSEDLY DEAD HEROES HAVEN'T COME BACK TO LIFE IN THE PAST. OUR CEMETERY IS PRACTICALLY AN OUTPATIENT PROGRAM.

YEAH, BUT THERE WAS ALWAYS A *TRICK*. THEY NEVER REALLY, YOU KNOW, CAME BACK FROM BEING ACTUALLY, LIKE, REALLY SINCERELY *DEAD*.

HM. YES. THAT'S THE THING, KEVIN.

THERE WAS ALWAYS A *TRICK*.

OKAY. DON'T *NO* ONE MAKE A BIG *THING* OF THIS.

IT DOESN'T *MEAN* NOTHING, ARE WE CLEAR ON *THAT?*

IT'S HIM. LET'S HAVE NO MORE FUSS ABOUT IT.

WHO WANTS MEATLOAF?

MY DEAR *GOD* IN *HEAVEN.*

UH, DISPATCH?

LISA, WE GOT AN E.T.A. ON THE SHERIFF'S RETURN? WE HAVE KIND OF...A *SITUATION* HERE, AND I COULD USE TOMMY'S...

TRUTH BE TOLD, TROY, I CAN'T RAISE HER *OR* PRESLEY ON THEIR RADIOS *OR* CELL PHONES. I'M GETTING A LITTLE NERVOUS.

THAT'S WEIRD.

SHALL I CALL THE STATE POLICE?

NAH, NO. SHE'S BRINGING BACK THE MAYOR. LET'S HANDLE THIS OURSELVES FOR NOW, OKAY?

OKAY, IF YOU'RE THE REAL MR. ARTICULATE, WHAT WAS THE *NAME* OF YOUR CHARACTER IN THE UNDERRATED CULT SENSATION *BEACH BUNNY BIKINI!!!*?

AH, I PLAYED THE DEATHLESS ROLE OF ONE CHESTERFIELD B. SMYTHINGSTONE, THE THIRD, EZEKIAL.

TROY, I'M FIXING TO GET WORRIED ABOUT MY HUSBAND...

I'M ON IT, SUZE. I PROMISE.

I WONDER IF I COULD ASK THE THREE OF YOU A *FAVOR*.

RECKON YOU MIGHT... SET ME *DOWN* A SPELL, SHERIFF?

IF... WHEW. IF YOU... INSIST, DEPUTY.

YOUR LEGS ARE BOTH BROKEN, PRESLEY. I SHOULDN'T OUGHT TO'VE MOVED YOU, BUT...

GOT SOME BROKEN GLASS INSIDE, TOO, I'M AFRAID. BUT BETTER BROKEN THAN BAKED, SHERIFF. NO APOLOGIES NECESSARY.

HE BETRAYED US, YOU KNOW. SET THIS ALL UP, HAD TO HAVE.

WE DON'T KNOW THAT.

SURE WE DO, SHERIFF.

AND YOU MIGHT WANT TO THINK ABOUT THIS. WE'RE ALONE OUT HERE WITH HIM.

AND YOU REMEMBER WHAT HE TRIED TO DO WITH THE *LAST* WITNESS AGAINST HIM, RIGHT?

I'D CHECK YOUR AMMO, SHERIFF. I SURELY WOULD.

GONE SOFT, I MEAN.

MAYBE THAT WOULD HAVE BEEN BETTER FOR US ALL.

I WANT YOU TO KNOW, I'M DOING THIS WITHOUT ANGER.

UGHHG.

I FIND ANGER TO BE SO...

...UNSANITARY.

YOU... WHAT DO YOU...

WHAT DO I WANT?

YOU'RE STRONG, MAYOR. YOU SAY YOU CAN LIFT A TANK, I SAY I BELIEVE YOU.

BUT YOU DON'T KNOW WHAT STRONG IS.

I COULD HURL THIS STATE INTO THE SUN, MAYOR.

I COULD CRACK THIS PLANET IN HALF. IT WOULD TAKE TIME AND EFFORT. BUT I COULD DO IT.

HEY!

BLAM BLAM BLAM

AIN'T ANGELS S'POZEDTA GRANT A DYIN' MAN A LAST REQUEST, DARLIN'?

YOU HUSH, YOU DIRTY OLE BIRD.

COSMOS, I WANT YOU TO TELEPORT JORDAN AND A COUPLE OF HIS E.M.T.'S HERE *NOW*, ALONG WITH ANYTHING THEY NEED TO GET PRESLEY STABLE, YOU HEAR?

RIGHT AWAY, SHERIFF.

YOU COULD HAVE JUST SHOT *NEAR* ME, TOMMY.

I NEEDED TO BE SURE YOU GOT THE MESSAGE, MAXI-MAN.

LISTEN. I NEED TO TELL YOU SOMETHING.

"SOMETHING'S OUT THERE. SOMETHING BIG ENOUGH TO USE A HUGE TREE LIKE A BASEBALL BAT.

"AND IT DIDN'T CARE IF WE LIVED OR DIED. AND KEVIN?"

EITHER THE MAYOR'S BEEN *KIDNAPPED*...

...OR HE'S *IN* ON IT. I NEED YOU TO FIND HIM.

AND BE PREPARED TO TAKE HIM *OUT*.

YOU DO.

YOU TRYING TO SCARE ME, SON?

I KNOW. YOU FOUGHT THE NAZIS A GILLION YEARS AGO.

IN THE BUCKET.

EXCUSE ME?

PAINT. MY HORSE. I PUT HIM IN THE *BUCKET*.

IT WOULDN'T EAT THE *APPLE* I BROUGHT. SO I SHOVED HIM IN THE BUCKET.

IT WAS *HARD*. IT TOOK *FOREVER*.

BET HE WISHES HE ATE THE APPLE *NOW*.

YOU LITTLE *MONSTER*.

WHAT ARE *YOU* MAD ABOUT?

IT'S JUST A STUPID HORSE.

I CAN BRING IT BACK.

...YOU...

YOU CAN DO THAT? BRING THINGS... BACK?

YEAH.

WOULD HE BE... WOULD HE BE WHOLE? LIKE HE USED TO BE?

NO. NOT LIKE HE USED TO BE.

NO.

WANT ME TO DO IT? IT'S KIND OF FUNNY IN A SAD WAY. FOR A WHILE.

NO. FOR GOD'S SAKES, NO.

COME UP TO THE HOUSE, SON. YOUR MOTHER'S WORRIED.

WE CAN TALK.

OKAY.

BUT SHE'D BETTER NOT BE *MAD* AT ME.

THEY'RE COMING FOR YOU, DAD.

THOSE GREAT *"FRIENDS"* OF YOURS.

LIKE THE STARS IN THE HEAVENS, AREN'T THEY?

ROYALTY OF THE MASK.

HOMECOMING part three
AN ARMOR of HISTORY

written by GAIL SIMONE   art by HORACIO DOMINGUES   colored by JONNY RENCH
lettered by TRAVIS LANHAM   asst. editor: KRISTY QUINN   editor: BEN ABERNATHY
cover: NEIL GOOGE & RENCH

YOU LOOK OLD TONIGHT, DAD. YOU FINALLY LOOK OLD.

PLEASE, SON. WE DIDN'T...

WE DIDN'T KNOW WHAT ELSE TO DO.

WHAT IS IT YOU WANT?

I WANT EVERYTHING YOU HAD. I WANT PEOPLE TO SPIT WHEN THEY SAY YOUR NAME. YOU WERE THE KING. I SHOULD HAVE BEEN THE PRINCE.

I WANT TO POUND SOME NAILS, DAD. I WANT MY THRONE.

AND I WANT SOME GIRLS. A LOT OF GIRLS. ALL THE GIRLS.

STARTING WITH MY UNFINISHED BUSINESS WITH THOMASINA, DAD.

IT'S ONLY FAIR. SHE OWES ME A GOOD TIME.

AND THEN, WHEN YOU SEE WHAT A DELIGHTFUL PARTY I'VE CREATED OUT OF YOUR LITTLE PEOPLE AND THEIR LITTLE LIVES...

...THEN I PUT YOU ALL IN THE BUCKET, "MAYOR."

GIVE MOM A SQUEEZE FOR ME, WOULD YOU?

HEY... HEY, IS THAT--

IT'S THE *MAYOR*, MAXI-MAN!

I *SEE* HIM!

GOOD WORK, GOSHAWK. SHARP EYES, LITTLE LADY!

YOU SAID HE COULD BE DANGEROUS, SHERIFF. SHOULD I SET YOU DOWN SOMEWHERE?

IT'S YOUR CALL, TOMMY.

...

I'M STILL THE LAW, KEV.

TAKE US DOWN.

MAYOR? ALEX?

ALEX, IT'S THOMASINA.

ALEX?

IT'S TOMMY, ALEX.

YOU WERE ALWAYS MY DAUGHTER, TOMMY. AFTER YOUR REAL DAD DIED...

I JUST WANT YOU TO KNOW, YOU WERE ALWAYS MY DAUGHTER.

DIDN'T MATTER WHO YOUR REAL DAD WAS. COLOR DIDN'T MATTER. NOTHING MATTERED. YOU WERE JUST LIKE...

NO. YOU WERE MY DAUGHTER.

I KNOW THAT, ALEX. I KNOW.

WE HAD TO CHOOSE, TOMMY. DEREK OR YOU.

WE CHOSE YOU.

TROY?

WE'VE FOUND THE MAYOR, DEPUTY. TELL PINK BUNNY.

TELL HER...

TELL HER HER HUSBAND'S COMING HOME.

COPY THAT, SHERIFF.

COPY THAT ALL OVER!

THEY FOUND HIM, SUZE. HE'S BANGED UP.

BUT HE'S COMING HOME.

THANK YOU.

THANK YOU, GOD.

THIS IS COMPLETELY UNNECESSARY.

OH, HUSH UP, OLD MAN.

"OLD MAN"? I'M TWO YEARS YOUNGER THAN YOU!

YEAH, BUT I LOOK YOUNGER.

LET'S NOT... LET'S NOT TALK ABOUT THAT RIGHT NOW.

SURE, ALEX. SURE.

HOT SOUP, COMIN' THROUGH! WE GOT WOUNDED, PEOPLE!

LET ME *BE*, TOMMY. I HAVE TO *SEE* HIM.

SUZE, NO. LET RACHEL AND JORDAN LOOK HIM *OVER* AND MAKE SURE THAT HE'S...

I KNOW THAT, SUZE. YOU COULD PUNCH ME TO PORTLAND. I KNOW.

IT'S JUST--

YOU CAN'T *STOP* ME, THOMASINA LUANNE LINDO!

--WELL, YOU WOULDN'T WANT TO RESIST AN OFFICER OF THE LAW IN FRONT OF KIDS, WOULD YOU?

WHAT SORT OF MESSAGE DOES THAT SEND?

ALL RIGHT, TOMMY. I'LL BEHAVE. FOR A *WHILE*.

BUT THEY'D *BETTER* HAVE SOME RECENT DAMN *MAGAZINES* IN HERE!

THERE AIN'T NO ONE ELSE LEFT, MISTER HENRY HATE, SIR.

THAT IS TRUE.

BE A SHAME TO LET ALL THIS BOUNTY GO TO WASTE.

THIS *ALSO* IS TRUE.

THERE NOW. FEEL BETTER?

I MUST SAY, SERESA LINDO. YOU'VE GROWN UP TO BE QUITE A JUICY MOUTHFUL. THOMASINA, TOO. I ACTUALLY *SAW* YOUR SISTER TONIGHT, YOU KNOW.

YOU LEAVE HER *ALONE*, YOU FREAK!

YOU ALMOST *KILLED* HER LAST TIME!

DID I? HMM. WELL.

YINKIES!

I'LL BE MORE *CAREFUL* THIS TIME.

AND THE *NEXT*.

AFTER THAT, WHO CAN SAY?

NOW, FORGIVE ME, BUT I HAVE A BIT OF A HEADACHE.

AND I'D APPRECIATE A BIT OF *QUIET*.

HMM.

IS THERE ANY MORE *PIE*, BY CHANCE?

RUN

PLS

YES, WORK THOSE SEXY LEGS, LITTLE GRANNY.

I'LL GIVE YOU THIRTY *SECONDS.*

THEN WE GIVE THE TABLOIDS SOMETHING TO *REALLY* TALK ABOUT!

TRANQUILITY HOSPITAL

ALL RIGHT, ALEX. I KNOW YOU KNOW WHO DID THIS.

THIS IS YOUR CHANCE TO REDEEM YOURSELF.

TOMMY, DAMMIT. I DIDN'T...

I DON'T *KNOW* HOW IT WENT SO WRONG.

IT FEELS LIKE EVERY ROTTEN THING THAT'S EVER HAPPENED TO THIS TOWN IS SOMEHOW BECAUSE OF *ME.*

I FEEL BAD FOR HIM.

I KNOW HE'S HURTING.

BUT I LOVE THIS TOWN. I SWEAR TO CHRIST, I DO.

I LOVE EVERY SILLY, RIDICULOUS PET, PERSON AND PLACE *IN* IT.

I WOULDN'T TRADE THE FISHING TOURNAMENTS AND SALMON BAKES FOR BROADWAY *AND* PARIS. THIS IS... IT'S MY *HOME.*

YOU HAVE TO *KNOW* THAT.

YOU HAVE TO *BELIEVE* IN ME AGAIN, TOMMY.

OR I JUST DON'T THINK I'M GONNA *MAKE* IT.

ALEX.

THOMASINA LUANNE LINDO FORGAVE YOU A GOOD WHILE BACK.

THAT'S NOT WHO YOU'RE TALKING TO, HERE. YOU UNDERSTAND?

ONE SECOND WHILE I GET THIS.

WE ARE *NOT DONE* TALKING.

BZZZT BZZZT

TMMY. HLP.

THINK.

THINK M DYIN.

SERESA?

SERESA?!!?

HE'S GOT MY SISTER.

OH, GOD.

NO.

LET ME GET MY DRAWERS ON.

NO.

HE ALMOST KILLED YOU *ALREADY.* AND HE HATES YOU LIKE A DOG HATES A *BATH.*

I NEED YOU TO STAY AND MAKE SURE HE DOESN'T COME AFTER *SUZE.*

BUT...

THAT'S AN *ORDER,* ALEX.

BUT IT'S...

IT'S ALL...

I FEEL BAD FOR HIM.

I KNOW HE'S HURTING.

IT'S ALL MY *FAULT.*

BUT I HAVE TO THINK OF MY *TOWN* RIGHT NOW.

OUR FATHER, WHO ART IN HEAVEN.

PLEASE GOD. PLEASE.

I RECKON THAT'S YORE WAY A *CALLIN'* ME, SHERIFF.

YES. YES.

WELP. YA *GOT* ME.

WHAT'S ALL THE *COMMOTION?*

ALL RIGHT. YOU'RE *DEAD,* RIGHT?

THAT I AM, MA'AM.

AND NOTHING, *NOTHING* ANYONE DOES TO YOU IS GONNA MAKE YOU, WHAT, ANY *MORE* DEAD, I GUESS, RIGHT?

I RECKON YOU AIN'T TRYING TO CHEER ME *UP* NONE WITH THIS LINE O' QUESTIONIN'.

KID. HE...

A RAPIST HAS MY SISTER.

...

SADDLE UP, SHERIFF.

I'LL DO AS I CAN, SUCH AS THAT MAY BE.

I LOVED THIS SAUCY LITTLE NUMBER.

I DON'T WANT YOU TO THINK OF THIS AS A *COMMITMENT*, MINXY.

IT'S STRICTLY ME REBELLING AGAINST... WELL. EVERYTHING!

YOU HURT *VENUS*, YOU ROTTEN *CRUMB-BUM!*

YOU'RE STARTING TO ANNOY ME, LITTLE GRANNY.

PUT YOUR LITTLE REMOTE *DOWN*.

IT'S NOT A REMOTE.

IT'S MORE LIKE A *DOG* WHISTLE.

AND *YOU'RE* THE STUPID *TABBY!*

MPHINXIES!

MISS MINERVA, WHERE'S SERESA? WHERE'S MY SISTER?

VENUS! SHE'S IN THE HOUSE, TOMMY!

WHERE IN THE HOUSE, MINXY?

SHE'S HURT BAD! SHE'S IN THE HOUSE!

MINXY. LISTEN TO ME.

I NEED TO KNOW. WAS SHE ON THE TOP FLOOR?

WHERE IS SHE?

OH. I REMEMBER. I REMEMBER NOW.

SHE'S DEAD, TOMMY.

I'M SO SORRY.

WHY, SURE, YOU WORTHLESS LI'L SQUIRT OF YOUR DADDY...

...THAT'D SUIT ME JES' PLUM SWEETLY.

ALL RIGHT, COWBOY.

GO AHEAD ON, THEN.

WHEN MONSTERS CLASH!

NO SIGHT, NO EXPERIENCE YOU CAN *IMAGINE* IS AS *FEARSOME*, AS *GRIMLY TERRIFYING*, AS WHEN HUMANITY IS FACED BY NOT *ONE*, BUT *TWO* NIGHTMARISH BEASTS, ON THE *PROWL* FOR THEIR *OWN UNKNOWN* PURPOSES! ONE WOULD *THINK* THAT FOR THESE BEINGS TO *FIGHT*, TO ATTEMPT TO *DESTROY* EACH OTHER, WOULD ONLY BE TO *EARTH'S BENEFIT!*

BUT WHAT IF IT ONLY MADE THINGS WORSE?

THE *HELPLESSNESS* OF THE BEAST'S *FORMER* POTENTIAL *VICTIMS!* WILL THE MONSTERS *DESTROY* EACH OTHER? OR WILL *ONE* OR *BOTH* SURVIVE TO *TERRORIZE* THE HAPLESS *WITNESSES?*

AT *FIRST!* THEY *CIRCLE* EACH OTHER... *TESTING* EACH OTHER'S *RESOLVE*, EACH OTHER'S *DEADLY FEROCITY!*

THE *TERRIFIED* TOWNSFOLK CAN ONLY *HOPE!* CAN ONLY *PRAY* TO THEIR VARIOUS *BELIEF SYSTEMS!* THAT THE ONE LESS BLOODTHIRSTY, LESS *HUNGRY* FOR *HUMAN PREY...*

...WILL *SURVIVE!*

TRANQUILITY HOSPITAL

I'M WAITING TO SEE MY DADDY.

EXCUSE ME?

HE BROKE HIS FOOT. FRACTURE. HE HAS A FRACTURE.

OH. I'M SORRY ABOUT THAT, SWEETIE.

I'M SURE HE'S FINE.

ARE YOU HERE TO SEE YOUR DADDY?

NO, HONEY. MY HUSBAND... HE HAD AN ACCIDENT.

BET HE CAUGHT A FRACTURE.

YOU LOOK SAD.

WANNA READ MY COMIC? I DON'T KNOW ALL THE WORDS, BUT IT'S MY FAVORITE.

MAXI-MONSTERS

12¢ MARCH 1960

MONSTERS, MONSTERS, MONSTERS!

IN THE DARK OF NIGHT, YOU WILL HEAR YOURSELF SCREAM!

OH, THANK GOODNESS, DOCTOR! THE CREATURES SEEM TO BE FIGHTING EACH OTHER!

I WOULDN'T BE TOO RELIEVED, PENNY! THEY ARE FIGHTING...

...US AS THE PRIZE!

CAN HUMANITY SURVIVE... WHEN MONSTERS CLASH!

FANGS, I MEAN, *THANKS*, FOR JOINING US ONCE AGAIN, FEAR, I MEAN, *DEAR* READER!

I'M YOUR OL' PAL, ZOMBIE *ZEKE*, AND THIS IS MY FRIEND *HAMNET*, AND WE HAVE A SCARY, I MEAN A *FAIRY* TALE THAT'LL MAKE A CHILLING, I MEAN *THRILLING* BEDTIME TALE!

WHEN MONSTERS CLASH!

NO SIGHT, NO EXPERIENCE YOU CAN *IMAGINE* IS AS *FEARSOME*, AS *GRIMLY TERRIFYING*, AS WHEN HUMANITY IS FACED BY NOT *ONE*, BUT *TWO* NIGHTMARISH BEASTS, ON THE *PROWL* FOR THEIR *OWN UNKNOWN PURPOSES!* ONE WOULD THINK THAT FOR THESE BEINGS TO *FIGHT*, TO ATTEMPT TO *DESTROY* EACH OTHER, WOULD ONLY BE TO *EARTH'S BENEFIT!*

OH, DOCTOR... IT'S HORRIBLE. *HORRIBLE!* *TWO* SUCH ABOMINATIONS!

WE CAN ONLY PRAY THAT *NEITHER* SURVIVES THIS CONFLICT, PENNY!

THE *HELPLESSNESS* OF THE BEAST'S *FORMER* POTENTIAL *VICTIMS!* WILL THE MONSTERS *DESTROY* EACH OTHER? OR WILL *ONE* OR *BOTH* SURVIVE TO *TERRORIZE* THE HAPLESS *WITNESSES?*

AT *FIRST!* THEY CIRCLE EACH OTHER...*TESTING* EACH OTHER'S *RESOLVE*, EACH OTHER'S *DEADLY FEROCITY!*

THE TERRIFIED TOWNSFOLK CAN ONLY *HOPE!* CAN ONLY *PRAY* TO THEIR VARIOUS *BELIEF SYSTEMS!* THAT THE ONE LESS BLOODTHIRSTY, LESS *HUNGRY* FOR *HUMAN PREY*...

...*WILL SURVIVE!*

WHY IS *THIS* COMIC YOUR FAVORITE?

IT SEEMS LIKE IT'D GIVE YOU NIGHTMARES, SWEETIE.

SEE, MOSTA THESE *OLD* COMICS AREN'T VERY SCARY, BUT THEY'RE ALL MY MOMMY LETS ME READ. NO ONE EVER DIES, YOU KNOW?

NO ONE EVER CATCHES A *FRACTURE*, EVEN.

BUT IN *THIS* ONE, IT'S DIFFERENT.

ON ACCOUNTA THE *ENDING.*

THE ENDING?

MONSTERS, MONSTERS, MONSTERS!

AND AS THE VICTOR LIMPS AWAY TO LICK HIS WOUNDS, THE VILLAGERS ARE FORCED TO ASK A HEART-BREAKING *QUERY!*

DID THE SO-CALLED "*CREATURE*" SACRIFICE ITS VERY *LIFE* TO SAVE THE PEOPLE WHO TRIED TO *DESTROY* IT?

DID IT DIE A *MONSTER*...

...OR A *HERO?*

SEE? IT'S NOT *REALISTIC* IF NOBODY *DIES*.

...AHUH. AHUH.

WELL.

YOU DID BETTER THAN MY OLD MAN, COWBOY.

GONNA HAVE TO HOLE *UP* FOR A BIT AFTER THIS.

SERESA COULD *STILL* BE ALIVE.

I CAN'T...I CAN'T STAY HERE AND FISH THE *KID* OUT.

HE'S DEAD ALREADY. I *KNOW* THAT.

JINKIES!

HE'S DEAD ALREADY.

THERE'S NOTHING I CAN *DO* FOR HIM.

DOODY.

I CAN'T JUST *LEAVE* HIM, SERESA.

NOT IF THERE'S A *CHANCE*.

I'M SORRY.

MINXY! YOU'VE GOT TO GET THE REST OF HIM OUT OF THE WATER, *FAST*.

CAN YOU DO THAT? MISS MINERVA, I NEED YOUR HELP!

JEEPERS, *ROGER* THAT, TOMMY!

...

WOMAN, WOULD YOU KINDLY... KLLK...

...QUIT YER FUSSIN' AND BLUBBERIN' AND GO *GET* YOUR LI'L SIS?

SERESA!

OH, MY GOD, OH, BABY.

I'M GONNA GET YOU OUT. YOU'RE FINE. YOU'RE OKAY.

I SAW HIM, TOMMY. DEATH.

I THINK... I THINK HE HAD A CRUSH ON ME.

WH OOOSHHH

I WAS TWELVE WHEN I FIRST MET HIM.

I DIDN'T KNOW. HOW COULD I KNOW?

WHY DO WE HAVE TO GO SWIMMING AT THIS CRAZY WHITE PEOPLE'S HOUSE, ANYWAY? THE SCHOOL GOTS A POOL.

BECAUSE EVERYONE PEES IN THE POOL, INCLUDING YOU, SERESA THERESE LINDO!

ONE TIME I PEED!

IF I'D KNOWN, I SWEAR. I SWEAR TO GOD AND MY DAD'S GRAVE--

--I WOULDA FOUND A GUN AND SHOT HIM 'TIL I RAN OUT OF BULLETS.

WHY, HELLO, GIRLS! AREN'T YOU BOTH ADORABLE?

HELP Y'ALL WITH SOMETHING?

BOOBIES.

UH...WE WERE EATING WITH OUR MOM AT YOUR RESTAURANT AND YOU SAID WE COULD COME BY ANY TIME AND SWIM IN THE LAKE AND BORROW YOUR PADDLEBOAT AND NEVER MIND WE'LL JUST GO, SORRY SORRY SORRY!

NONSENSE, BLACK GLIDER'S GRANDKIDS ARE WELCOME ANYTIME! WHY DON'T I MAKE YOU UP SOME BIG FAT CHEESEBURGERS FIRST? PADDLING TAKES A MESS OF ENERGY.

WHY, WE SEEM TO HAVE A COUPLE LOVELY YOUNG LADIES VISITING!

YOU TWO GO ON DOWN TO THE BOATHOUSE AND I'LL MAKE YOU SOME LUNCH.

'LO, MAYOR FURY.

BE...CAREFUL, ALL RIGHT?

WE'RE BIG GIRLS, MISS SUZY.

I THOUGHT SHE MEANT THE WATER. BE CAREFUL OF THE WATER.

SUZE, WE CAN'T...WE CAN'T LET THEM SEE HIM.

LIKE FUN WE CAN'T, ALEX. THIS IS JUST WHAT HE NEEDS.

TO PLAY, AND TO BE A KID FOR ONCE.

BUT THAT'S NOT WHAT SHE MEANT AT ALL.

OH. HELLO.

...

UM. HI, HELLO, I MEAN.

I'D LIVED IN TRANQUILITY ALL MY LIFE. SUZY'S FRIED CHICKEN WAS THE MOST FAMOUS THING IN TOWN, REALLY.

BUT NEVER ONCE HAD I HEARD THEY HAD A *SON*.

AND UNSURPRISINGLY, GIVEN HIS PARENTS...

...HE WAS CUTE LIKE A *HOUSE* AFIRE.

I'M TO... THOMASINA.

I'M JUST DEREK.

TOM-MY'S GOT A *BOY-FRIEND!*

HAHAHAHAHA!

HEY. WAIT. *NO FAIR!*

SO, UM... YOU LIVE HERE OR SOMETHING STUPID?

YEAH.

DO YOU LIKE PONIES? I HAVE A PONY NAMED PISTOL. I USED TO HAVE ONE NAMED PAINT, BUT... HE DIED.

DO YOU WANT TO GO SEE HIM?

WHAT THE DOODY? NO ONE I KNEW EVER HAD NO *PONY*.

YES! I MEAN... ...SURE, THAT'S COOL. WHATEVER.

DANG NABBITGOD DANGDOODY STUPIDBIG SISTERWITH HERDUMB FACEHEAD!

THAT DAY, THAT DAY WHERE I NEVER QUITE MADE IT TO THE PADDLEBOATS, HE WAS JUST A BOY.

HE SEEMED ALMOST *TOO* EAGER TO PLEASE.

ALMOST *TOO* NICE.

I FELT SORRY FOR HIM. IT WAS LIKE HE WAS A TEST SUBJECT, INSTEAD OF A *KID.*

SO YOU DON'T HAVE TO GO TO *SCHOOL?*

NO.

I WISH I DID, THOUGH. SCHOOL SOUNDS COOL.

MAYBE YOU GOT BRAIN DAMAGE, SAYING A THING LIKE THAT.

PRETTY.

ARE YOU SAD, 'CAUSE YOU DON'T HAVE ANY FRIENDS OR ANYTHING?

SOMETIMES.

I GOT TO GO TO THE MOON, ONCE. DAD KNOWS SOME GUYS AT NASA.

OKAY. HERE'S THE DEAL.

I'LL BE YOUR FRIEND. AND YOU CAN HOLD MY HAND. *A LITTLE.*

TRY TO KISS ME AND I'LL BELT YOU ONE.

AND IF MY MOM SEES US, I DON'T KNOW YOU.

GOT IT?

OKAY. NOW SHOW ME HOW TO DRIVE THIS CRAZY DOODY THING.

WE'RE GOING *RIDING.*

I'M NOT GOING TO LIE TO YOU, SHERIFF.

THE PROGNOSIS IS A LITTLE BIT GRIM.

JUST TELL ME, DOCTOR MORRISON.

ALL RIGHT, TOMMY.

SHE WAS RIGHT AT THE BRINK OF CATASTROPHIC BLOOD LOSS AND HER HEART RATE WAS HUGELY ACCELERATED TO COMPENSATE.

IT'S A RAGGED WOUND, 2CM WIDE, OF THE SKIN AND SUBCUTANEOUS TISSUES OF THE LATERAL NECK. BOTH THE INTERNAL AND EXTERNAL JUGULAR VEINS WERE LACERATED.

"LOOKS TO HAVE JUST NICKED THE CAROTID...THAT'S A BIT OF LUCK. CUT THE STRAP MUSCLES UP PRETTY BAD, THOUGH.

"THE PHRENIC AND LANYNGEAL NERVES APPEAR INTACT, BUT WE'LL NEED TO..."

I DON'T CARE ABOUT THAT. IS SHE... IS SHE GONNA BE HERSELF WHEN SHE WAKES UP?

SCOTT, LISTEN. TOMMY'S BEEN THROUGH A LOT. CAN WE POSSIBLY...

I UNDERSTAND. IT'S THE FORK, RACHEL.

IT RESTED ON THE SPINAL CORD. WE CAN PURSUE AN AGGRESSIVE TREATMENT SCHEDULE INCLUDING STEROIDS, BUT RIGHT NOW...

...WELL, SHE'S LIKELY TO EXPERIENCE PARAPLEGIA.

I HOPE IT'S TEMPORARY.

TOMMY, REALLY, THE ODDS ARE GOOD THAT...

I GOT IT, RACHEL.

THANK YOU.

KNOCK, KNOCK, PRESLEY.

SHERIFF *LINDO*. YOU DIDN'T BRING NO *BEER*, DID YA?

GAMEKID

GAMES

MAYOR FURY VS. MAXIMAN

ASKED MY *NIECE* TO BRING ME A SIX O' FURY *LITE*, AN' LOOK AT WHAT SHE BRUNG ME *INSTEAD*.

DANG *KID'S* GAME OR *CELL PHONE* OR SOME DAMN SUCH.

I'LL SEE WHAT I CAN DO.

DEREK HURT SERESA REAL BAD, PRESLEY. YOU KNOW WHAT HE IS.

I WANT YOU TO MOVE INTO HER ROOM WHILE SHE'S HERE.

AND ONE OTHER THING.

WELL, SURE, SHERIFF. I...

TAKE THIS. HIDE IT. BUT KEEP IT CLOSE.

NOW, TOMMY, YOU KNOW BULLETS AREN'T GONNA SLOW HIM *DOWN* IF HE COMES FOR HER.

I KNOW.

IF HE COMES FOR HER, YOU'LL HAVE ONE SHOT, IF YOU'RE LUCKY.

YOU TAKE MY SISTER OUT *CLEAN*, HEAR?

TOMMY?

WHAT IS IT, AJITA?

IT'S THE RESTAURANT, TOMMY. THE CHIK-N-GO. IT'S CLOSED.

"BUT IT'S SUPPOSED T' BE OPEN.

"AND PINK BUNNY NEVER GETS SICK. NOT EVER."

AND ALEX, MAYOR FURY... HE'S LEFT HIS HOSPITAL ROOM.

I THINK THEY'RE GONE, SHERIFF.

I THINK THEY HIT THE TRAIL AND ARE GONE.

DOC TOMORROW.

NEED A HAND, HERE, MISTER.

WHAT DO YOU HAVE THAT CAN KILL A GOD?

I SHOULDA CANCELED THE CONCERT.

BUT MAYBE HAVIN' ALL THE TOWN'S MAXIS *TOGETHER* WILL KEEP DEREK AWAY.

I SHOULDA CANCELED THE SHOW.

TROY, YOU DON'T KNOW WHAT THIS GUY IS LIKE.

CLEAR SO FAR, SHERIFF. LOTTA OUT-OF-TOWNERS, BUT NO ONE SEEMS TO BE OF A MIND TO CAUSE A RUCKUS.

YOU EVEN *THINK*, YOU EVEN HAVE A SECOND'S *DOUBT* ABOUT ANYONE, YOU POLITELY PULL THEM FROM THE CROWD.

BUT CALL ME *FIRST*.

NO OUTSIDE ALCOHOL, NO VIDEO, NO FLASH, MAN.

'SOKAY IF I PISS IF MY BLADDER GETS FULL, FOOL?

HEY, YOU OKAY, SHERIFF? YOU NEED SOME WATER OR SOMETHING?

I'M FINE, TROY.

BUT I WASN'T FOR A WHILE. I WASN'T FINE AT ALL.

NOT AT ALL.

I DIDN'T TELL MY MOM AT FIRST.

THAT WAS BREAKING HER *STRICTEST* RULE.

BROKE THE RULE ABOUT *KISSING*, TOO.

BROKE THAT RULE ALL TO PIECES.

AT FIRST IT WAS FUN, HAVING A SECRET BOYFRIEND.

MOM'S GONNA FIND *OUT*.

NOT IF YOU DON'T TELL HER, SERESA.

I AIN'T NO *SNITCH*, THOMASINA LINDO!

AND HE REALLY *WAS* THE PERFECT BOYFRIEND.

HANDSOME AS THE DEVIL, AND TWICE AS STRONG.

AND FAITHFUL?

WHO WOULD HE CHEAT WITH?

NO ONE EVEN KNEW HE *EXISTED*.

YOU WANT ONE OF THOSE STARS?

I'LL GET IT FOR YOU. JUST SAY THE WORD.

HA! YEAH, THE NORTH STAR. I'LL HAVE THAT ONE, PLEASE.

HEY... WAIT. YOU'RE KIDDING, RIGHT?

SURE. GUESS SO.

I MISSED OUT ON THINGS. TALKING ABOUT BOYS TO MY FRIENDS. MY PROM. THE SADIE HAWKINS DANCE.

I DIDN'T CARE. I WAS IN LOVE.

AND I WAS GOING TO BE A *COP*.

AND THE MAN I WAS GOING TO MARRY WAS GOING TO BRING ME A STAR SOMEDAY.

THEN, THREE *DAYS* AFTER GRADUATING FROM THE POLICE ACADEMY, I GOT THE NEWS THAT I KNEW WAS GOING TO RUIN EVERYTHING.

THREE DOODY *DAYS*.

HEY. C'MON. WHATEVER IT IS, IT CAN'T BE *THAT* BAD.

DEREK.

I'M *PREGNANT.* WE'RE GONNA HAVE A *BABY*.

COME ON, DEREK. IF YOU'RE NOT DEAD, SHOW YOURSELF. NO MORE AMBUSHING PEOPLE IN THE NIGHT.

I'M NOT RUNNING FROM YOU ANYMORE.

AND YOU WON'T TAKE MY SISTER...

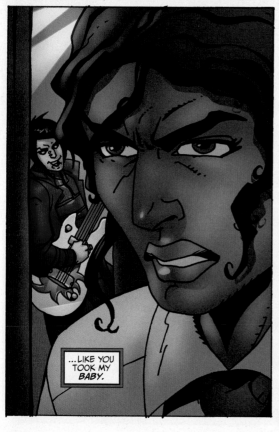

...LIKE YOU TOOK MY *BABY*.

OH, HOW NICE. THEY'VE PUT ON A *SHOW* FOR ME.

MAYBE I'LL GIVE THEM SOMETHING TO BE EMO *ABOUT*.

ER.

I TRIED TO CHANNEL UP A RAVEN BUT HE CAME DOWN LAME BLOODY DOGS IN THE STREET LICKED MY HAND AND MADE ME TAME AND THE HERO TAKES A BULLET IN THE BEST AND FINAL FRAME WHILE MY SEXY SUPER FRIENDS SAY THEY'VE GONE AND LOST THE GAME AND MY SEXY SUPER FRIENDS SAY THEY'VE WENT AND LOST THE GAME...

IT'S NOT JUST ME, IS IT?

THEY REALLY ARE DREADFUL, YES?

AW, I DON'T KNOW WHAT THESE KIDS GOT TO GRIPE ABOUT *ANYHOW*, MR. ARTICULATE.

IT AIN'T LIKE THEY GOTTA FIGHT THE *NAZIS*.

I'M JUST WAITIN' FOR ZOMBIE ZEKE, TO BE HONEST.

DID I MISS ANYTHING? DID THEY PLAY "UNDEAD AND UNCONCERNED" YET?

GAH!

I'VE BROUGHT HOT DOGS.

NO, *THANK* YOU.

THEY'RE FOR ME, A. *THANKS*, COSMOS!

WE WERE JUST DISCUSSING HOW THIS, EH, "MUSIC" IS NOT MUCH TO OUR TASTES, I'M AFRAID?

REALLY? I'M A BIG FAN. THESE KIDS REALLY *SPEAK* TO ME SOMEHOW.

HE'S OUT THERE. DEREK IS. I COULD ALWAYS FEEL HIM.

LIKE A WASP AT A PICNIC.

WE WERE IN LOVE.

WE WERE GOING TO BE MARRIED.

EVEN THOUGH I ALREADY *KNEW* THERE WAS SOMETHING HORRIBLY *WRONG* IN HIS BRAINPAN.

DEREK. I'M *PREGNANT*.

WE'RE GONNA HAVE A *BABY*.

A... WAIT. A BABY?

MY SEED?

DO YOU *KNOW?* DO YOU *KNOW* THE THOUGHTS...

...THE THINGS THAT GO THROUGH MY *MIND?*

DO YOU THINK I WANT ANOTHER... ANOTHER LIKE *ME?*

I THINK, ALL THINGS CONSIDERED, YOU WANT TO LIVE, YOUNG LADY.

I WOKE UP IN THE HOSPITAL, WITH MR. ARTICULATE BY MY SIDE.

SAYING THE ONLY THING IN THE WORLD THAT MADE ANY SENSE TO THE KNOT-HEAD I HAD BEEN UP TILL THAT POINT.

MY MOTHER AND SISTER CRIED FOR DAYS.

BUT IT WAS MR. A'S COMMENT THAT KEPT ME EATING, KEPT ME FROM THE DARKNESS.

KEPT ME FROM THINKING ABOUT WHAT WAS, AND WHAT IS, AND THINKING INSTEAD ABOUT WHAT *COULD* BE.

ALEX AND SUZE CAME BY WITH THE SAD BUT INEVITABLE NEWS.

DEREK HAD DIED IN THE STRUGGLE.

"I THINK, ALL THINGS CONSIDERED, YOU WANT TO LIVE, YOUNG LADY."

I WOULDN'T HAVE SURVIVED WITHOUT THAT.

WHEN I GOT OUT, I WENT STRAIGHT TO HIS HOUSE TO THANK HIM. WHICH I DID.

ABOUT SEVEN *TIMES* THAT NIGHT.

THE BUNNY AND FURY LIED ABOUT DEREK, OF COURSE. HE WAS NEVER DEAD, JUST SE[NT] AWAY TO A SPECIAL GOVERNMENT PRISO[N].

AND MR. A IS BACK FROM THE DEAD, SOMEHOW, TOO.

IN GOD'S NAME, *HOW?*

IT'S ALMOST TIME FOR ZEKE TO TAKE OVER THE STAGE, SHERIFF.

MAYBE HE'S NOT COMIN'?

YOU DON'T KNOW HIM, DEPUTY TROY VERRILL.

HE'LL BE HERE.

HE HAS UNFINISHED BUSINESS.

AND PEOPLE TO PAY *BACK.*

AND *ME.*

BUT ALL THINGS CONSIDERED?

I WOULD RATHER *LIVE.*

ALL MY GANGSTAS AND GORGEOUS FINE *THINGS* IN THE HOUSE, GIVE IT UP FOR MY *MAN.*

HE *DEF.* HE *DED.* HE GOT A *SHOVEL* AN' A *SNAKE* AND HE *ALWAYS* ON THE MAKE!

PUT IT TOGETHER FOR...

I'M SORRY, MY TOWN, MY PRECIOUS SMALL, SILLY TOWN.

THAT I HOLD SO DEAR TO MY HEART.

PLEASE FORGIVE ME.

I'VE MADE YOU BAIT.

AND THE BIG ONE IS COMING TO BITE.

I'M SO SORRY.

THERE WAS NO OTHER WAY.

MAYOR! MAYOR *FURY.*

COLLETTE?

I THOUGHT I'D FIND YOU HERE.

YOU'D BETTER GET OUT OF HERE, COLLETTE. SOMETHING... SOMETHING VERY BAD IS ABOUT TO HAPPEN.

NO. NO! IT DOESN'T *HAVE* TO HAPPEN! PLEASE. HE'LL *KILL* YOU. HE *WANTS* TO KILL YOU!

"HE FOUND ME, MAYOR."

HELLO, COLLETTE.

"HE *MADE* ME RECANT MY TESTIMONY. SAID HE... HE WANTED YOU TO TASTE *FREEDOM* ONE LAST TIME."

I'M SO, SO SORRY.

YOU DON'T APOLOGIZE TO ME, COLLETTE. NOT AFTER...

...NOT AFTER THE MISTAKES I MADE.

BUT I *KNOW* YOU'RE A HERO INSIDE! THAT'S WHY I DID IT!

DARLIN', I'M NOT ANY KIND OF HERO.

BUT BLESS YOU FOR SAYING THAT.

MAYBE I CAN GO *OUT* RIGHT, IN ANY CASE.

NO!

DEREK!

I'M CALLIN' YOU *OUT*, BOY!

WELL, WELL, WELL.

FATHER AND CHILD REUNION.

ONLY EMOTION AWAY.

IMAGINE. THAT. WHAT.

A NIGHT.

FOR IT.

TOO.

YOU THINK YOU DIE IN GLORY, OLD MAN? DON'T YOU GET IT?

DON'T YOU SEE WHY YOU HAVE TO DIE, AND IN *SHAME?*

IT'S BECAUSE I AM YOUR *SON!*

YOU LET ME THINK YOU WERE *GOOD.* YOU WERE A *HERO* AND I WAS THE ROTTEN PIECE OF *PULP* STUCK TO YOUR *DENTURES!*

BUT YOU WERE BAD ALL ALONG!

YOU *MADE* ME WHAT I AM! IT'S *ALL YOUR FAULT!*

I COULD HAVE KILLED YOU ANY TIME, DAD.

BUT THERE'S SOMETHING I WANT YOU TO SEE FIRST.

THERE'S A CONCERT.

IT'S NOT... IT'S NOT FAAAAIRR!

THANK GOD. IT'S OVER.

IT'S OVER.

AND MIRACULOUSLY, NO MORE BLOODSHED.

OH, LORD. ALEX.

STEP ASIDE, EVERYONE.

THIS IS MY DUTY.

ALEX, WAIT. HANG ON. WE DON'T HAVE TO--

DOC TOMORROW MADE THIS GUN, SON. IT'S A CHRONOLOGICAL AUTOMATIC.

IT UNMAKES THINGS.

I'M SORRY.

YOU IMBECILE! DON'T YOU GET IT? DON'T YOU UNDERSTAND WHAT I HAVE DONE?

I COULDN'T LET THAT BABY BE BORN. I COULDN'T LET...LET SOMETHING LIKE ME BE BORN!

DON'T YOU SEE? DON'T YOU SEE WHAT I STOPPED FROM HAPPENING?

I'M THE GREATEST HERO IN HISTORY!

A HERO!

GOD HELP ME.

I CAN'T DO IT.

I SAVED EVERYBODY! I'M A HERO, DAD!

I'M JUST LIKE YOU!

I WISH, I WISH IT IDN'T TURN OUT THIS WAY. CONSIDERING WHAT DEREK DID, THERE'S NO QUESTION PINK BUNNY WILL GET OFF WITHOUT SERIOUS CHARGES.

BUT THE FURY NAME IS DONE. WHATEVER GOOD THEY'VE DONE, HATEVER KINDNESSES... ALL ANYONE ON THE OUTSIDE WILL EVER REMEMBER IS SHE SHOT HER OWN KID.

I'M SORRY, SUZE.

ALEX SAID THAT DEREK COULD BRING THINGS BACK TO LIFE, IF HE CONCENTRATED. SAID IT WAS IMPOSSIBLY HARD, BUT HE COULD DO IT.

DID HE BRING MR. A BACK BECAUSE HE KNEW...KNEW HOW I FELT ABOUT HIM?

WAS THIS A GIFT? A TORMENT? A TEMPTATION?

I DON'T KNOW. BUT MR. A CAME UP AND MADE SURE I WAS OKAY, FIRST THING, WHILE EVERYONE ELSE WAS STILL WONDERING WHAT HAPPENED.

I DON'T KNOW HOW I'M GOING TO EXPLAIN TO MAMA THAT I WANT TO MARRY A SEVENTY-FIVE-YEAR-OLD WHITE MAN WHO MAY OR MAY NOT BE A RE-ANIMATED CORPSE.

BUT I DO.

AND I'M GONNA.

THE HEART WANTS WHAT IT DAMN WANTS.

SHE'S GONNA BE OKAY.

WIN SOME, LOSE SOME, KID.

GOT A LITTLE REGULAR CHORE UP THE COAST I HAVE TO DO FIRST.

THEN, OH, YES, THEN.

OREGON

BECAUSE ALL THINGS CONSIDERED, I WANT TO LIVE.

OH, YES, I DO.

WOULDN'T MIND SEEING WHAT THE MAN LOOKS LIKE IN SOMETHING OTHER THAN FORMAL EVENING WEAR, MIND YOU.

HOWEVER MUCH TIME WE BOTH HAVE LEFT. IT'LL HAVE TO DO.

IS THAT...?

THAT'S THE HOUSE, YES.

BUT THERE'S *TIME* FOR THAT.

I WAS EIGHTEEN YEARS OLD. MY BOYFRIEND WAS A SUPER-POWERED PSYCHOPATH. I WAS INJURED BADLY.

YOU COME *STRAIGHT* HOME FROM THE LIBRARY, ALEX. YOU UNDERSTAND ME?

I WILL, MOM!

NO ONE KNOWS BUT PRESLEY, MY MOM AND SERESA.

I DIDN'T LOSE THE BABY. NOT TO *MISCARRIAGE*, LIKE I TOLD EVERYONE, ANYWAY.

BE GOOD, SWEETIE.

I WILL.

LOVE YOU, MOM.

I KNOW ADOPTION WAS THE RIGHT THING. BUT I COME UP AND CHECK ON HIM EVERY SO OFTEN. HE'S HAPPY. HE'S CONTENT.

SO FAR, HE RESEMBLES *MY* SIDE OF THE FAMILY.

THANK GOD.

THANK GOD.

HOMECOMING
part six

ENDING NOTE

written by GAIL SIMONE   art by HORACIO DOMINGUES
colored by CARRIE STRACHAN   lettered by TRAVIS LANHAM
asst. editor: KRISTY QUINN   editor: BEN ABERNATHY
Cover by NEIL GOOGE & JONNY RENCH
Dedicated to the memory of JONNY RENCH:
An amazing artist, friend, and brother.